A Life in Politics

AL GORE

by Rebecca Stefoff

JEFFERSON SCHOOL
FOURTH AVENUE
DIXON, ILLINOIS

A Gateway Biography
The Millbrook Press
Brookfield, Connecticut

Cover photo courtesy of Liaison Agency (© Alex Wong)
Background cover photo courtesy of Superstock

Photos courtesy of: AP/Wide World Photos: pp. 6, 9, 14, 19, 21
(top), 22, 30, 34, 39(bottom); UPI/Bettmann: 10; Sygma: pp. 13,
21 (bottom), 25, 26, 37,(Mike Stewart); The White House: p. 39 (top).

Library of Congress Cataloging-in-Publication Data
Stefoff, Rebecca, 1951–
Al Gore: a life in politics / by Rebecca Stefoff.
p.   cm.—(A Gateway biography)
Includes bibliographical references and index.
ISBN 1-56294-433-9 (lib. bdg.) 0-7613-1329-X (pbk.)
1. Gore, Albert, 1948– —Juvenile literature. 2. Vice
Presidents—United States—Biography—Juvenile
literature. {1. Gore, Albert, 1948– . 2. Vice-
Presidents.] I. Title. II. Series.
E840.8G65S74   1994
973.929'092—dc20   [B]   93-13850   CIP   AC

Published by The Millbrook Press, Inc.
2 Old New Milford Road
Brookfield, Connecticut 06804

Al Gore

One April day in 1989, Al Gore took his six-year-old son, Albert, to a baseball game. They went to see the Boston Red Sox play the Baltimore Orioles in Baltimore.

It was an exciting game. Young Albert especially enjoyed seeing Cal Ripkin, the Orioles' star shortstop. But the afternoon was much more than a pleasant outing for Al Gore and his family. It became a turning point in all their lives.

After the game, the Gores left the stadium and walked across a parking lot. Albert held his father's hand and talked happily about the game. Suddenly he slipped away, as children sometimes do, and ran ahead. Without looking where he was going, he ran right into the path of a car. The car hit Albert and left him lying on the pavement.

Al Gore ran to his son's side. He could see that Albert was badly hurt. He was not even sure that the boy was still alive. He held his son and prayed while he waited for the ambulance to come.

Young Albert was not dead. He had been seriously injured, and he had to have several operations and stay in the hospital for a long time, but he

Al and Tipper Gore leave Johns Hopkins hospital with Albert. The experience of almost losing his son left a deep impression on Al.

lived. He began to heal. A special operation was needed to fix his right arm, which had been damaged in the accident, but after the operation he could use the arm as well as ever. A few years later, he could even pitch a softball at 50 miles an hour.

But in the dark days and nights right after the accident, Al Gore did not know if his son would ever get well. He and his wife, Tipper, spent thirty days and nights in the hospital, watching at Albert's bedside.

The walls of Albert's room were covered with hundreds of cards and letters wishing him well. Some of the cards were from friends of the Gore family. But others were from people who had never even met young Albert. They had heard about the accident on the news, because Al Gore was a well-known public figure. He was a United States senator from the state of Tennessee. Many people outside Tennessee had heard of him, too, because he had tried to become president of the United States just a year earlier.

While Al Gore sat in the hospital room watching his son sleep, he had time to think about many things. He thought about what he had achieved during his life, and about what he still hoped to do. He thought about young Albert and Albert's three sisters, and about all the other children in the world. What kind of future would they have? Would the earth be a safe, comfortable home for them when they grew up?

For years, Al Gore had studied the environment. As a teenager, he had read *Silent Spring,* by Rachel Carson. In the book, Carson talked about the chemicals used by farmers to protect their crops from insects. She warned that these poisons were killing many kinds of animals, fish, and birds. Later, during the Vietnam War, Gore had seen American soldiers use even more powerful chemicals to kill trees so that the enemy could not hide in them. He had traveled through country "that used to be jungle but now looked like the surface of the moon." He had wondered: Do we really know what we are doing when we spray these poisons into our air?

Later still, Gore had seen the earth's rain forests being cut down. He had learned that the climate all over the world was slowly getting warmer because of the chemicals that cars and factories

U.S. Air Force planes spray Agent Orange, a chemical that causes the leaves to drop off plants, over the Vietnamese countryside. Gore was horrified to learn that Vietnam's plant and animal life might never recover.

Gore also became concerned over damage to the environment in the United States. In this photo of Denver, Colorado, only tall office buildings and mountains rise above a layer of pollution.

breathe into the atmosphere. He knew that our rivers and oceans were getting more polluted every day, and that many kinds of birds and animals were disappearing forever as their homes were destroyed. Like many other people, Al Gore had begun to worry about the way we were changing the earth's environment.

Now, young Albert's close brush with death caused Al Gore to think about the things that were most important to him: his family, his hopes for his children's future, and the future of all living things on this planet. He also remembered his own childhood.

Al Gore was born on March 31, 1948, in Washington, D.C. His full name was Albert Arnold Gore, Jr., but he was always called Al, and his father was called Albert, Sr. Al's parents both came from small towns in Tennessee, but Al was born in Washington because his father's office was there. Albert, Sr., was a congressman for many years. Al learned a lot about politics and government from his father.

Al was the second child born in his family. His

sister, Nancy, was ten years old when he was born. The *Tennessean,* a newspaper from Albert, Sr.'s, home state, said that when Al was born, Nancy called "everybody in the telephone directory" to tell them the news. In spite of the difference in their ages, Al and Nancy were good friends from the start.

As a boy, Al had two homes. For part of each year, the Gores lived in a hotel in Washington. The rest of the time, they lived on the family farm near Carthage, Tennessee. Al Gore liked the country better than the city. Years later he said, "If you're a boy, and you have the choice between the eighth floor of a hotel and a big farm with horses, cows, canoes and a river—it was an easy choice for me."

Young Al had many good times on the farm. He explored the river in his canoe, and he learned to ride a pony. On hot days, he went swimming in the cows' water trough with his friend Gordon, whose parents were caretakers on the farm. Al and Gordon loved playing with Gordon's dog, Patsy. One day Patsy disappeared. The boys were heartbroken, but Al refused to stop looking for Patsy, even after the grown-ups had given up hope. Ev-

The Gores enjoy a canoe ride down a river on their farm sometime in the 1950s. Al's sister, Nancy, sits in the bow; he and his mother, Pauline, are in the middle; and his father, Senator Albert Gore, Sr., is paddling the boat.

Life in Washington, D.C., was a far cry from the casual freedom at the Carthage farm. Here, nine-year-old Al kisses his mother goodnight as his parents leave for a White House reception.

eryone was surprised and happy when Patsy was found a few days later. She had gotten stuck in an old building, but she was alive and well.

Life on the farm was not all play and pets, however. Al Gore learned that farming was hard work. He hoed the tobacco patch, harvested the corn crop, and looked after the livestock.

He also learned about taking care of the land. He saw that rain flowing in little gullies could wash away the soil that made the land good for farming. With each rainfall, the gullies got bigger, and more precious soil was washed away. To stop this erosion, careful farmers filled in the gullies with stones. Al Gore remembered this lesson later, when he began thinking about how people were damaging the environment. He often used the example of the gullies and the stones to show that people *could* take action to stop problems before the problems got out of control.

Al went to school in Carthage at first. When he got a little older, he went to St. Albans, a boys' school in Washington. As a teenager, he liked to come to the farm to visit his Tennessee friends, to fish and swim and water-ski. But there was a lot to do in Washington, too. His parents made sure that he went to museums, art galleries, concerts, and plays. They wanted him to enjoy one of the world's great cities as well as country life.

School kept Al very busy. He studied hard and got good grades all the way through high school at St. Albans. Besides studying the required subjects of math, history, and English, he got to choose some courses for himself. He chose classes in painting and writing.

Al Gore played football and basketball for St. Albans. In his senior year, he was the captain of the football team. He also served in the student government. When he graduated in 1965, the St. Albans yearbook said under his picture: "It probably won't be long before Al reaches the top."

Something special happened to Gore when he graduated from high school. At a graduation party, he met a lively young woman with blond hair who lived in Arlington, Virginia, close to Washington. Her name was Mary Elizabeth Aitcheson. She had been known as Tipper ever since she was a baby because her mother used to sing her to sleep with a song called "Tippy Tippy Tin."

Al liked Tipper so much that he called her the very next day to ask her for a date. Tipper was impressed with the tall, dark-haired boy. He was smart and interesting as well as good-looking. She agreed to go out with him, and soon they were spending a lot of time together.

In the fall of 1965, Al Gore started college. He had been accepted at Harvard University, one of the best schools in the United States. When Tipper graduated from high school the following year, she chose a college in Boston so that she could be close to Gore.

The two young people continued to date. Then, in 1967, Tipper paid her first visit to the Gore farm in Carthage. It was a memorable occasion.

Al Gore had prepared a special present for Tipper. It was a baby skunk, with its scent glands removed so that it could not produce the awful smell for which skunks are famous. Tipper loved the silky little animal and made a bed for it in a box. But the skunk chewed a hole in the box and escaped. Tipper was so upset that Al searched the garden for the skunk. Finally he found it and brought it into the house — but he had found the wrong skunk! Everyone ran out of the house as the new skunk let off its strong scent bomb.

Gore worked hard during his four years at Harvard, where his main field of study was government. He spent one summer taking classes in Mexico City, where he learned to speak Spanish. Another summer was spent working for the *New York Times*. Gore was becoming interested in writing, and he wanted to learn about newspapers. Perhaps he would become a reporter.

Gore's years at Harvard were a time of great change and confusion in America. The United States was fighting the Vietnam War in Southeast Asia, but many Americans, especially many young people, felt that the war was wrong. They did not think that U.S. troops should be sent to Vietnam. Students at many colleges protested against the war by seizing control of buildings or staying away from classes. Some young men broke the law by refusing to sign up for the draft, the system by which they would be drawn into the armed forces.

Al Gore believed that the Vietnam War was wrong, but he felt torn. Although he did not want to support the war, he had too much respect for the

This was one of many protests against the Vietnam War in Washington, D.C. Despite his personal belief that the war was wrong, Gore felt that it was his duty to serve.

law to break it. And his father, who also disapproved of the war, was struggling to stay in the Senate. If Al Gore tried to avoid the draft, he could hurt his father's chances for re-election.

Gore wrestled with this problem. He knew that other young men, including friends he had grown up with, were facing enemy bullets in Vietnam. How would he feel if he refused to serve his country in a time of war?

Finally, Gore's sense of duty outweighed his feelings against the war. In the summer of 1969, he joined the army. He was sent to an army base in Alabama and given a job on the base newspaper.

The following spring, Al Gore and Tipper Aitcheson were married in Washington, D.C. They set up their first home in a trailer in Alabama. Six months later, Gore was ordered to Vietnam, where he served for about half a year.

The war had a deep effect on Gore, as it did on most of the Americans who went to Vietnam. Gore did not fight any battles. He was a combat journalist. His job was to write about the war for army newspapers. But he saw enough action to convince him that violence is not how human beings should

Newlyweds Al and Tipper Gore share a happy moment with Al's parents.

Six months later, Al was sent to Vietnam as a journalist. This photo shows him adjusting a gun strap.

Millions of people were killed during the civil war that raged in Vietnam from 1957 to 1975. Here, civilians huddle together in shock, caught between enemy troops. Al Gore was changed by what he saw there.

settle their differences. He wrote to friends that he was haunted by the horrible things he had seen.

Gore *returned* to the United States in 1971 and settled down with Tipper in Carthage. He bought some land there and started his own company to build and sell houses. But real estate was not enough to hold his interest. He began thinking about what he wanted to do with his life.

Religion had always been important to Gore. As a child, he went to Baptist church services with his parents. Now he enrolled in divinity school at Vanderbilt University in Nashville, Tennessee. Divinity school prepares people to become ministers, but Gore was not set on becoming one himself. He just wanted a chance to think about religion. He wanted to ask important questions about life and death, good and evil. Divinity school did not give Gore all the answers he looked for, but he said that it taught him to ask "better questions."

In the meantime, Gore returned to writing. He found work as a reporter on the *Tennessean.* Tipper Gore went to work for the *Tennessean,* too, as a photographer. Soon the Gores moved to Nashville to be closer to the newspaper offices. Their first child, a daughter named Karenna, was born there in 1973. Three more children followed: Kristin in 1977, Sarah in 1979, and Albert III in 1982.

Al *Gore was a fine writer,* and he could have made a name for himself in the newspaper business. His favorite stories were those in which he exposed shady deals or bad government. As time went on, though, Gore wanted to do more than write about these problems. He wanted to help solve them. In 1974 he started law school at Vanderbilt University. He had begun thinking about a career in government.

Earlier, Albert Gore, Sr., had urged his son to enter politics, but Gore did not let his father direct him. Although he respected his father's views, he wanted to make up his own mind. But now his mind and his heart told him that he was ready for public service.

Al Gore decided to run for Congress in 1976 — for the same seat that his father had first won

Al with Tipper and their four children in 1984.

Al Gore campaigns for Congress in 1976. The people from his district in Tennessee elected him four times to represent them. He worked hard, and he meant what he said.

thirty-eight years before. If the people of Tennessee voted him in, Gore would become a member of the House of Representatives.

He made his first campaign speech on the courthouse steps in Carthage. Then he walked down the street, shaking hands with everyone he met and asking them to vote for him. He felt very awkward at first. But after he had shaken hands with ten or twelve people, his confidence grew, and he started to feel more comfortable.

Gore won the support of the Democratic party, and on election day he saw that the people believed in him, too. He won his first election, and he was re-elected to the House three times. He served in the House of Representatives for eight years in all.

During those years, Gore built a reputation for hard work and honesty. Unlike some representatives, he rarely missed a vote or other important House business. He also found time to return to his district almost every weekend to meet with the people who had elected him and listen to their concerns. In eight years, he held 1,600 of these meetings — more than any other representative in history.

Gore did a lot of good in the House of Representatives. Many of his projects dealt with health. He helped pass laws that forced cigarette and liquor companies to put stronger labels on their products warning about the health hazards of tobacco and alcohol. He worked on plans to help the homeless and people with AIDS. He worked to pass laws making it illegal for companies to sell baby food that did not meet health standards.

In 1980, Gore made a speech at a girls' school in Tennessee. He was shocked when nearly all of the girls said that they thought there would be a nuclear war in their lifetimes. This made him sad and angry. What a horrible way to grow up, expecting worldwide destruction at any moment!

Gore began to study the nuclear arms race. He learned so much about it that even people in the Republican party, who did not like to praise Democrats, said that Gore was one of the top nuclear experts in Congress. Gore encouraged President Ronald Reagan, and later President George Bush, to make deals with the Soviet Union that would allow both countries to destroy some of their nuclear bombs and still feel safe.

The environment was of special concern to Gore. In 1978 a family in Tennessee wrote to him saying that chemicals dumped near their farm had made them sick. Gore found that several million gallons of hazardous waste had been dumped into ditches in that part of the state. The waste was leaking into people's wells and poisoning their water.

Gore set up meetings in Congress to make the other representatives aware of the problems of toxic waste dumps. These were the first meetings that had ever been held on the subject of toxic waste. As a result, two years later Congress passed a law creating the Superfund, which set aside government money to clean up the worst toxic waste dumps. Gore was one of the authors of that law.

He also brought up the subject of global warming. Every time people burn oil, coal, or gasoline, carbon dioxide enters the air. Some scientists believe that this causes a "greenhouse effect" that makes the Earth warmer. In time, this global warming could melt the polar ice. Cities and towns on seacoasts all over the world could be flooded.

Gore spoke about global warming to the members of Congress. There were angry debates on the

Congressman Gore leads a meeting about the danger of toxic waste dumps. He was well aware of the terrible effect that chemicals could have on plants, animals, and people, and he was not about to sit back and let it happen.

subject. The oil and coal companies and the carmakers dismissed global warming as nonsense. Some scientists also claimed that global warming had not been fully proved. But Gore felt the evidence for global warming was strong. He believed that we must stop adding "greenhouse gases" like carbon dioxide to the air, or we'll change the Earth's climate. He used an old Tennessee saying to make his point: "When you're in a hole, stop digging."

In 1984, Gore ran for a seat in the U.S. Senate. He went to Tennessee to ask people to vote for him. He liked to talk to them face-to-face, but sometimes that was impossible. One day he was driving along a country road when he spotted a parked truck. A man was underneath the truck, working on the engine. Gore knelt down, introduced himself, asked for his vote—and then shook the man's ankle because he couldn't reach his hand.

In the middle of his campaign, Gore received tragic news. His beloved sister Nancy, who had been a heavy smoker, was dying of lung cancer. Gore spent hours at Nancy's side during her last days. He was deeply shaken by her death, but carried on with his campaign and won more votes than any other candidate in the history of Tennessee.

In the Senate, Gore continued to work on health care, education, nuclear arms control, and the environment. But after a few years he began thinking about the next step in his political career. He believed that the country needed a big change in leadership, and he knew that he had good ideas to offer. After long talks with his family, he decided to run for president in 1988.

Other hopeful Democrats had the same idea, however. More than half a dozen of them competed in state primary elections. The Democrats chose Michael Dukakis, the governor of Massachusetts, as their candidate for president that year. Gore returned to the Senate.

Then, in the spring of 1989, came young Albert's accident and the long hours that Al Gore spent thinking about the future. In his son's hospital room, Gore began writing a book. He described a trip he had taken to the South Pole, where he watched scientists measure the damage that people had done to the Earth's atmosphere.

He wrote about a visit to the Amazon River in Brazil, where the sky was black with plumes of smoke from the burning rain forest. Gore also told of a murdered elephant he had seen in Africa. Its ivory tusks had been sawed out of its head by illegal hunters.

Gore called his book *Earth in the Balance.* He hoped that it would make people think about protecting the Earth and its fragile riches instead of using them up and destroying them. "We must all become partners in a bold effort to change the very foundation of our civilization," he wrote. Many people, including some scientists, disagreed with the information and ideas Gore expressed in *Earth in the Balance.* Still, the book became a best-seller and won Gore the support of people in the environmental movement.

The Democrats chose Bill Clinton, the governor of Arkansas, as their candidate for president in 1992. Gore thought that Clinton would make a good president. Clinton liked and admired Gore, and he knew that Gore was an expert on the en-

Senator Gore talks to a homeless man during his unsuccessful run for president in 1988.

vironment and defense, among other subjects. He asked Gore to be his running mate, and Gore agreed. Four years after his failed attempt to be president, Al Gore was running for vice president.

He and Clinton made an impressive team. The two young men, both from the South, took on the Republican party and President George Bush. Clinton debated the president, and Gore debated the vice president, Dan Quayle. Crisscrossing the country in buses, Clinton and Gore promised to make changes in the way government worked.

Clinton promised to heal America's ailing economy and to create jobs for the growing number of jobless workers. Many Americans liked this message. Environmental groups, too, supported the Democrats because Gore was part of the team.

And the voters responded. In November 1992, Bill Clinton and Al Gore won a strong victory. In January 1993, they were sworn into office as the president and vice president of the United States.

The vice president's job has always been hard to define. Some vice presidents have been very active. Others have done almost nothing. But President Clinton made it clear that Gore would have some very important responsibilities.

One of Gore's jobs was serving as the head of the Senate, a task that every vice president has performed. Gore had plenty of other duties as well. Clinton put him in charge of all the government's programs and committees that dealt with the environment, energy, and new technology. The president also gave Gore a challenging special assignment called "reinventing government." He told Gore to spend six months surveying the entire federal government, looking for ways that the government could work better and spend less money.

It wasn't long before Al Gore had earned a reputation as one of the hardest-working vice presidents in American history. People in government—even those who were against Gore and his ideas—admired his energy and his intelligence.

Every week Gore and President Clinton shared a private lunch, a time when they could talk about issues in the news and about the country's future. Gore also went to many of the president's meetings. Clinton respected Gore's knowledge of complicated

When Gore visited Antarctica in 1971, scientists were measuring the pollution in Earth's atmosphere. He became even more convinced that we must try to save our environment.

subjects and his ability to make tough decisions. One White House official called Gore "the strongest and steadiest adviser that the president has."

One of Gore's most important jobs was building strong relationships with some other countries. He went to South Africa for the inauguration of Nelson Mandela, that country's first black president. After his meetings with Russian leaders, the United States and Russia began working together on energy, technology, and space programs. Later Gore visited China to discuss relations between the United States and China.

Closer to home, Gore's "reinventing government" project had some success. Gore cut costs in many government departments, but Republicans in Congress said that his reforms didn't save as much money as he had claimed they would.

In 1996, Bill Clinton and Al Gore campaigned for re-election against Bob Dole and Jack Kemp, the Republican candidates for president and vice president. One of the strongest moments in the Democrats' campaign came when Gore debated Kemp on issues such as foreign affairs and the econ-

Right: 1992 Democratic candidate Bill Clinton asked Al Gore to be his running mate. The two men toured the country in buses during the campaign.

Below: Gore speaks to the press following a meeting with Palestinian leader Yasir Arafat in 1998. The meeting was part of the ongoing struggle for peace between Palestinians and Israelis.

omy. Most viewers agreed that Gore won the debate. A few months later, the Democrats won the election, and Clinton and Gore began four more years as the country's top leaders.

Both men faced difficulties during their second term. Questions about Clinton's personal life led to an impeachment, a special kind of trial in which the president is judged by members of Congress. Congress found Clinton not guilty, but his misbehavior and the impeachment embarrassed the Democratic party.

Gore was accused of a different kind of wrongdoing in connection with raising money to pay for the 1996 campaign. It seemed that he had made telephone calls from his White House office asking for contributions, which is against the law. He faced hard questions about his possible connection to illegal campaign contributions, but he continued to do his job as vice president.

The eight years of the Clinton-Gore administration brought growing use of the Internet in education, business, and personal life. Gore approved of the Internet's growth and spoke of the day when all American homes, schools, and libraries would be able to share the wealth of information that it offers. As vice president he helped shape a Telecommunications Act that made it easier for the Internet to operate.

Gore also remained concerned for the world environment. Many environmentalists criticized him for not doing as much to protect forests, air quality, and endangered species as they had hoped he would do. Yet carmakers and other business leaders called him a "green" politician who put the environment ahead of jobs and business interests.

Gore's years as vice president gave him experience in trying to balance the needs and desires of different groups. In 2000, with his time as vice president drawing to an end, he put that experience to use in one of the greatest challenges of his life—a presidential campaign.

Twelve years earlier, Al Gore had tried and failed to become the Democratic party's candidate for president. Now, after two terms as vice president, he was the party's choice to run for president. He chose Joseph Lieberman, a senator from Connecticut, as his vice presidential candidate.

During the campaign, Gore and Tipper and daughter Karenna crisscrossed the country making speeches to voters. Gore's Republican opponent was George W. Bush, governor of Texas and son of former president George H. Bush. A consumer-rights spokesman named Ralph Nader ran as the presidential candidate of a smaller political organization called the Green party.

The Democrats hoped that voters would elect another Democrat because the country's economy had done very well during Clinton's time in office. Some of them, however, worried that Nader would draw votes away from Gore. But no one could have predicted what actually happened when Americans went to the polls in November.

The election of 2000 was one of the closest in American history—so close that television news broadcasters, trying to be the first to announce who had won, kept making mistakes. At one point it seemed that Bush was going to win, so Gore called him on the telephone to concede, or give up, the contest. Then, when more counting showed that Gore might win after all, he called Bush back to "un-concede." Gore was not willing to give up the fight until he was sure that he had no chance to win. But he did have one big disappointment during that long night. Tennessee, Gore's home state, favored Bush, as did most southern and western states.

Across the nation, more Americans voted for Gore than for Bush. Gore won 50,158,000 popular votes, Bush 49,820,000. But popular votes do not elect the president—the states' electoral votes do. Florida was the turning point. Each candidate needed Florida's electoral votes in order to win the overall election. When Florida's popular votes were counted, Bush won by 975 votes, which gave him all of Florida's electoral votes. But the result of the Florida vote was so close that Gore asked for a recount.

The recount lasted for five weeks, with legal procedures and court challenges on both sides. Questions were raised about voting machines and counting methods in Florida and elsewhere. Many people called for election reforms to ensure fairness in future contests. As the days dragged on, some said that Gore should give up the fight. However, he believed that the Americans who had voted for him deserved someone who would do everything possible to make their votes meaningful. Finally, though, the U.S. Supreme Court halted the recount, and Florida's electoral votes went to George W. Bush. Al Gore admitted the painful truth. The contest was over, and he had lost.

On December 13, 2000, Gore made a televised speech conceding the election. "This is America—and we put country before party," he said. "We will stand together behind our new president." Gore also said, "The strength of American democracy is shown most clearly through the difficulties it can overcome." Those words also describe Al Gore. His strength has allowed him to survive difficulties and setbacks and to keep working for what he believes is right. He will surely keep doing so in the future, whatever it may hold.

Important Dates

1948	Albert (Al) Gore Jr. is born on March 31 in Washington, DC.
1969	Graduates from Harvard University and joins the army.
1970	Marries Tipper Aitcheson and goes to Vietnam to serve as a combat reporter.
1971-1973	Goes to divinity school and works as a reporter on the *Tennessean*.
1976	Is elected to the House of Representatives.
1984	Runs for the U.S. Senate and is elected. His sister, Nancy, dies of cancer.
1988	Tries to become the Democratic party's choice for president but loses to Michael Dukakis. He returns to the Senate.
1989	Gore's son, Albert Jr., is hit by a car and almost killed.
1992	Publishes *Earth in the Balance* and is elected vice president.
1996	Bill Clinton and Al Gore are re-elected as president and vice president.
1998	Gore's father, Al Gore Sr., dies.
2000	Runs for president as Democratic party candidate. Wins the popular vote but loses the electoral vote to Republican George W. Bush, who is declared president

Further Reading

Al Gore: Leader for a New Millennium by Laura S. Jeffrey (Enslow Publishers, 1999).

Al Gore: United States Vice President by Betty M. Burford (Enslow Publishers, 1994).

Bill Clinton: President of the 90's by Robert Cwiklik (The Millbrook Press, 1997).

Picture This: A Visual Diary by Tipper Gore (Broadway Books, 1996).

The Story of Bill Clinton and Al Gore: Our Nation's Leaders by Kate McMullen (Gareth Stevens, 1996).

Tipper Gore: Voice for the Voiceless by JoAnn Guernsey (Lerner Publications, 1994).

Index